COLD FURY

The Cannock Chase Murders
David J Cooper

COLD FURY

First edition. March 21, 2020.

Copyright © 2020 David J Cooper.

ISBN: 978-1393327004

Written by David J Cooper.

Also by David J Cooper

Penny Lane, Paranormal Investigator
The Witch Board
The House of Dolls
The House of Dolls
The Devil's Coins
The Mirror
The Key
The Reveal

Standalone
Foul Play
The Devil Knows
The Party's Over
Penny Lane, Paranormal Investigator. Series, Books 1 - 3
Encuentro Mortal
Se Acabo La Fiesta
Cold Fury

Watch for more at davidjcooperauthorblog.wordpress.com.

Table of Contents

For my sister, Diane Worwood

Introduction

CHILD KILLERS DON'T have horns and tails. They look and act like you and me. But there is one key difference: they're sexually attracted to children. And we had one living on our doorstep.

It was the swinging sixties and I was part of it, a mod with shoulder length hair, riding around on a blue and white Lambretta SX 200 motor scooter and wearing bold print bell bottom trousers with little bells sewn on at the bottom, so while I was walking I'd be jingling.

I remember the Cannock Chase murders very well as I was living in that area at the time.

Cannock Chase, sprinkled with camping and caravan sites, is very popular at weekends with people from Birmingham and the Black Country.

I remember the police finding the bodies of two little girls there in 1966 but I was in Walsall town centre on the same afternoon in August 1967 when little Christine Darby went missing.

I remember all the police road blocks as I was returning home and wondered what had happened.

In 1973, Carol Morris, the murderer's now ex-wife, came to work as a wages clerk at the same local bicycle manufacturing company where I worked.

I became good friends with her and she came to my first wedding, in 1974, with her boyfriend.

I didn't realise who she was until I read an article in the Sunday Mirror which showed her photo.

She was a very attractive young woman and had a lovely personality. It was hard to believe that she had been married to a child killer.

She never mentioned her ex-husband to me but did say to me once that she had experienced a very traumatic time in her marriage which left her in a psychiatric hospital in Plymouth for six months.

I left the area in 1988 and the last I heard of Carol was that she got married again and had a baby boy and was still living in the area, working as a cashier at the local ASDA, a large supermarket chain.

It has taken me two years of research for this book which I hope you will find interesting. I hope you will leave a review.

Chapter 1

THE STRANGER'S HAND tightened on her arm, white knuckled and strong. Turning to fight it, ten year old Margaret found her feet dragging along the ground as she lost her balance. He was dragging her towards his car.

She strained her vocals but nothing came out, still she screamed, hoping someone would hear her.

Only a few minutes before, she and her nine year old brother, Stephen, had been helping their mother put the finishing touches to a bonfire on some wasteland on the corner of Bridgeman Street and Queen Street, Walsall, not far from the town centre.

It was 4th November, 1968.

"Stevie wants to go to the toilet," her mum said, taking hold of his hand. "Carry on throwing the rest of those twigs and dried leaves on the bonfire and we'll have it finished when I get back."

The bare skeletons of the trees shivered in the crisp, autumn breeze and a few dried up leaves rolled across the ground.

It was eight thirty in the evening but the waste land was pitch black. The street lamps on either side of the road radiated a warm orange glow, flickering in an attempt to light up the place.

Her old duffle coat, friendly and soft, was keeping her warm and the extra thick wool on her knitted mittens made her hands look larger than usual.

She didn't hear the green and white Ford Corsair pull up a few yards away.

A man got out of the car and pushed the door shut without making a sound.

Taking a few steps forward he paused, letting his eyes roam up and down the street making sure nobody noticed he was there. He knew what he wanted and this way his mind had a few moments longer to prepare.

Each step took him closer to the waste ground and closer to Margaret.

A slight and startling tingle tiptoed down her spine as she heard the crunch of dried leaves behind her. She turned abruptly.

Her heart was in her mouth as she saw a man appear from the shadows.

He looked as though he was in his late-thirties. His hair was done very nicely; he had some form of oil mixed in to give a short but noticeable wavy form. His forehead was almost square, large and imposing. A few lines were laid upon it, but they were dismissive as tricks of light. His eyebrows were impossibly straight, his eyes dark and penetrating. They were eyes that held many secrets. It just looked as if he had a secret you wouldn't enjoy hearing about.

His cold fury burnt with dangerous intensity.

"I didn't mean to frighten you," he said. "I noticed making a bonfire and thought you might like some free fireworks. I've got some in my car. Come along and I'll show you."

Once again fear found her. It spoke to her in its cackling voice. It told her legs to go weak, her stomach to lurch and her heart to pound like a drum. Her mother always told her not to speak to strangers. There was nothing to fear but fear itself, but still she could not silence its voice.

She tried to ignore him but he insisted she go with him.

"My car is just over there," he said. "It'll only take a few minutes."

As Margaret's worry grew and grew something drew her attention on the other side of the street.

Out of the fish and chip shop stepped a figure so bundled in a thick jacket that she couldn't tell if it was a man or a woman. As things turned out, the face peeking out of the parker was a young woman of about eighteen. Her cheeks were blanched from the cold and her eyes partially obscured with mousey hair.

The woman, Wendy Lane, noticed the man struggling with Margaret and sensed something wasn't right.

She called out, "Hey, what's going on over there?"

Her shouting was violence in the air. Its resounding shattered the silence of the street. She didn't just raise her voice, her muscles tensed for maximum impact as her hands squeezed at her packet of fish and chips.

He jumped back as if a firecracker had gone off and his face fell faster than the speed of light. In that instant his skin became greyed, his mouth hung with lips slightly parted and his eyes were as wide as they could stretch. He glanced nervously at his car.

Like a slippery eel, Margaret wriggled from his grasp and ran towards Mrs Lane. She breathed in and out but nothing would enter her lungs. Starved for air, her heart raced at tremendous speeds, and her chest shallowly rose and fell in time. She ran for what felt like an eternity but it was actually only a couple of minutes.

There was only one thing he could do and that was to get away. His foot nearly slipped from beneath him as he jumped in his car. Holding his head down over the steering wheel, he drove off erratically down the street.

Mrs Lane managed to memorise the number plate, colour, and make of car.

This was going to be the biggest mistake he'd ever made in his life.

Chapter 2

THE GREY SKY RESTLESSLY grumbled. The thick blackened clouds were dragged down by the heavy rain which it held in its delicate frame. The clouds, which struggled to withstand the burden of the weight which the rain held, soon gave in. It poured down over Malefant Street, in the Cathays area of Cardiff, with a roar. Other than that, it was a normal day for the Stephens family.

It was Tuesday, 7th April 1959.

For Carol, who was 6 years old, tall and plump with a fresh complexion, rosy cheeks, and brown hair, which always seemed to fall over her steel rimmed glasses, happiness was simple; hugs with her mom, Mavis, and playing in the street with her friends.

"Carol," her mum called. "It's stopped raining now. Go to the corner shop and get me a packet of ten cigarettes."

Handing her a half-crown coin she continued, "Here's the money. Just tell Mrs. Jones they're for me. She knows what sort I smoke. You can buy yourself some sweets with the change."

Carol hopped from one foot to the other. The saliva in her mouth had already pooled in her mouth as she thought about the sweets. She skipped down the street screaming with delight, whooping into the frigid air.

Her friend, six year old Kevin Northcott, stopped scribbling in his scruffy, little red notebook, turned and looked at her.

The corner shop was more of a club house for gossiping grannies than a shop, but Carol loved it better than anywhere else. The old ladies spoiled her. She could spend the whole weekend in there if her mom let her.

"Hello, Carol," said Mrs. Jones. "Have you come for some sweets?"

"My mom wants a packet of ten cigarettes," she replied, placing the half-crown coin on the counter. "She said I can have some sweets with the change."

"Here are the cigarettes," Mrs. Jones said, handing her a packet of Woodbine. "Put them in your pocket. I don't want the police seeing you with cigarettes. You have tuppence change."

"What can I buy with tuppence?" she asked.

"Let me see," she replied. "You can have two Penny Arrow toffee bars or eight Black Jacks."

"I'll have the Black Jacks," she said, licking her lips.

Mrs. Jones dropped the Black Jacks into a paper bag and handed them to her.

"Thank you," Carol said, smiling. As she was leaving the shop she noticed a green car parked by the kerb on the opposite corner. She immediately recognised it as the same car of the man who had told her he was her uncle. She ran back down the narrow road, bordered on each side with identical terraced houses with small upper windows, narrow porches and square bay windows.

"Here's your packet of cigarettes mommy," she said, handing them over. "I'm going outside now to play with Kevin."

She ran back outside and headed towards Kevin who was still busy scribbling in his notebook. Stepping into the puddles left by the rain, she wet her light brown shoes and splashed the water over her grey skirt and grey woollen jumper.

"What are you doing Kevin?" she asked. "I'm taking down car numbers," he replied, waving his notebook at her. "You know I like collecting them."

He was the same age as Carol and lived next door to her. There was something about him that she liked. He was quiet, but not out of being timid. He was reserved but not aloof. It was as if he was the type to observe the lay of the land before he got involved in anything.

Rustling the paper bag, she offered him one of her Black Jacks.

"My new uncle's around the corner in his car," she said. "He's been taking me for some lovely rides. I'm going to see if he'll take me for one today. Do you want to come?"

"No," he replied, taking a Black Jack.

She scurried down the street towards the corner shop once more, going out of sight as she turned the corner.

The dark haired man, about thirty years old, was sitting in his car reading some papers. He was wearing a long, double breasted coat with wide lapels. His head was tilted forward so she couldn't see his face properly because the black, brimmed hat he had on was pulled down.

Her fingers tapping on the window caught his attention.

"Hello, Carol," he said, opening the passenger door and contorting his lips into an awkward toothy smile. "Do you want to come for a ride?"

"Yes, please," she giggled.

"I'll take you for a long ride into the countryside today," he said. "Come on, jump in."

It was almost teatime and the rain had started falling heavily again.

"I'll have to go and call Carol in," her mum thought. "She's going to get soaked."

She opened the front door and called into the street.

"Carol, Carol, come on love. I don't want you getting wet."

She looked up and down but there was no sign of her.

On hearing the shouting, Kevin's mum popped her head out of the window.

"Are you looking for Carol?" she asked.

"Yes," she replied. "Is she with your Kevin?"

"No," she replied. "Kevin came in out of the rain and told me she's gone for a ride with her uncle."

"What uncle?" she asked.

"I don't know," she replied. "Kevin said that Carol asked him if he wanted to go for a ride with her in her new uncle's car. That's all I know."

The fear thoughts looped around Carol's mum's mind until there was no room for anything else. She went back into the house and called the police.

They were concerned, not just because a child had gone missing, but from the information they'd been given by Kevin and other neighbours. Carol's mother had also told them that she was a friendly little girl and would talk to anybody however much she discouraged her. All they had to go on at this moment in time was that Carol had asked Kevin to go with her for a ride in her uncle's car.

A neighbour had seen her get out of a car a few days before. She said that she thought it strange that the driver had dropped Carol off around the corner and not outside her house. A sixteen year old boy also told the police that he saw her getting into a green car that afternoon.

The clock was ticking away and the police knew that the longer the search for Carol went on the chance of finding her alive and well would diminish. However, the huge search for her was in vain.

After days of rain-washed streets, the owner of a nearby culvert in the small village of Horeb, sixty miles away from Carol's home, had asked a surveyor to unblock it because it had become covered by overhanging leaves and branches.

The water leaving the culvert had formed a babbling stream. Around it the greenery was drinking and fallen leaves had become boats. The sound of the water upon the rocks sang with a steady confidence to the chorus of the birds.

Half covered in wet leaves lay the form of a child, so still that he thought it was a doll. A few seconds later he blinked and jumped, moving backwards until his back hit a tree. A small gasp escaped his lips as they trembled. He realised that it was a little girl. Her flesh was as cold as the mud she lay in; her now pale skin was splattered and her face half submerged in the gritty muck. Her brown hair was dirty and her lungs were choked with sludge because her killer hadn't made any effort to see whether she was really dead when he dumped her body in the water, so she had breathed the stuff in with her last gasping breaths.

Her grey skirt was around her feet and one of her light brown shoes was lying five feet away from her. The other one was further downstream. Purple welts were scattered across her thighs and abdomen and there was a sharp edged band of purple-black across her nose and mouth that showed where the killer's hands had restrained her.

It was the 21st April; exactly two weeks after Carol had disappeared.

Chapter 3

IT WAS TIME. THE TIME she knew would come sooner or later but it was now nine o' clock and eight year old Julia Taylor knew it was time for her to go home. Her friend's birthday party had been fun, but all good things come to an end.

Night had fallen and enveloped the neighbourhood in a blanket of darkness.

She scurried along the pavement at a steady pace, her mind focused on the gentle footsteps that seemed to echo through the desolate street. Other than the darkness, which swirled around her, all that seemed to exist was the harsh bite of the chilly wind she could feel through her fur lined coat. The wind ruffled her simple white dress and the cold painted her cheeks bright red.

It was December 1st, 1964.

As her house came into sight, she saw the doorway light was on, and the familiar yellow glow of the lights inside made the house feel warm and inviting. To anyone else it was a house like all the others exactly like it on the street, but to her it was a sanctuary.

She noticed a man standing beside a grey car parked a few doors away. As she got near he turned around.

"Hello," he said. "Don't you remember me?"

"I don't think I do," she replied.

"I'm your uncle Len," he said. "I've just come to let you know that your mom is at your auntie's house and I've come to take you there to get some Christmas presents."

"I don't remember having an uncle Len," she said.

"Never mind," he said, opening the car door. "Get in and we'll be there in no time. It isn't too far away. Come on hurry up or your mom is going to start getting worried."

"Where is my mom?" she asked.

"I told you she's at your auntie's house in Bentley," he replied.

She got in the car and he drove off passing by her house.

After about ten minutes he pulled the car up onto a grass verge on the side of the road. It was pitch black and she couldn't see anything out of the car window.

"Why have we stopped?" she asked.

"Look," he replied, and started touching his genitals.

Her hands trembled and her eyes watered as she reached for the door handle.

"Please let me out," she begged. "Please let me go home. I want my mommy."

He sat there in the darkness of the car watching her eyes for the fear he'd longed to see, feeling a sick sense of joy rise within him. Opening the door, he pushed her out onto the grass verge.

As she cried her bottom lip quivered. She sank to her knees, not caring for the damp mud that dirtied her dress or the bitter cold gnawing at her legs.

She felt her throat tighten as she tried to take short intakes of breath. She could feel his fingers digging into her cheek; the four blackened ovals that would remain and discolour her skin long after the blood had dried.

He stifled her scream. She could hear him panting, the pleasure in his breath, like an animal on heat. He was not stealing but rather claiming what he thought was rightfully his. He didn't speak. There was no need to tell her not to fight or make a sound. His fingers did all the work.

Her eyesight became vague, but not because tears were brimming. Everything became blurred; then she saw nothing at all. Her awareness was floating through an empty space filled with a thick static. Throughout the inky space her heartbeats thumped loudly, echoing in her ears. The feeling in her body sapped away until finally all was black.

That was how she was to remain, silent, raped and left to die.

The lights of his bicycle, shining like smudged stars, caught the shape of a large car driving away. The wintry breeze blew cold kisses upon his face.

From the grass verge he heard a low, pitiful whining sound. The noise was somewhat spooky, perfect for the location. At first he thought it must be an injured animal lying in the grass; a few seconds later he realised that the noise wasn't coming from an animal but from a little girl choking, but miraculously she was still alive.

Chapter 4

THE RAIN KEPT ON COMING that Wednesday afternoon, the streets were utterly soaked as six year old Margaret Reynolds was returning to school in Whitehead Road, Aston, Birmingham, after a lunch break at her home in Clifton Road.

It was only a nine minute walk away.

The rhythm of the rain bounced upon her umbrella, each drop a clear beat upon the green fabric. As her fingers tightened around the curved wooden handle, a tiny smile grew wider.

Drops cascaded from the umbrella rim as pretty as any waterfall. She let herself watch them, water playing with the cloud-filtered light. It gave the city street a magical feeling, as if it were another world.

After a few minutes walking with her sister, Susan, they got to the corner of Albert Road.

"Hurry up to school, Margaret," Susan said, kissing her on the cheek. "I'll see you at home later."

She left Margaret and ran in the opposite direction to the secondary school she attended.

Holding her umbrella close to her head, so that her blonde hair wouldn't get wet, Margaret carried on walking towards the Prince Albert primary and infants school which was now in sight.

On the centre of the table top was a large, brown glaze teapot. The handle expanded outward almost as round as the pot itself, making it easy to take hold of and pour.

Florence Reynolds eyes kept darting from it to the clock. It was almost five o'clock and Margaret still hadn't returned from school.

"Where on earth can she be, Bill?" she asked.

"Maybe she's sheltering from the rain," Margaret's dad replied, tapping his fingers loudly on the table.

"I'm going to phone the school and ask if she's there," her mother said.

She returned quicker than she had left.

Running her hand through her hair, teeth tugging at her lower lip and tears streaming from her eyes, "We have to call the police," she said. "Margaret didn't turn up for school this afternoon."

Margaret's dad could feel it, building like an unstoppable snowball in the pit of his stomach. He couldn't concentrate on anything else. His heart started to beat harder and faster, his balls tried to crawl up inside his body and his brain started to fire out negative thoughts. The thoughts kept coming like waves on rocks. He was walking around back and forth.

It was September 8th, 1965.

Within hours, two thousand people were searching for her, but the intense police hunt ended, without a trace of Margaret being found.

Diane Tift, a cheerful and friendly child, traipsed along Chapel Street, Blakenall. Walsall, clasping her little brown handbag, which had been a Christmas gift, while her eyes were following a bird in flight in the grey washed sky. She watched as children do, with that look of love and awe.

Around her shoulders was her scarf, her chestnut fringe poking out from her pixie hood. Her camel coloured coat was keeping her warm. She had eyes that shone like pebbles washed by the ocean waves and a smile that ignited her inner laughter.

She had just left her grandmother's house and was now on her way home in Hollemeadow Avenue, only five minutes' walk away.

Her mum always made home-made stews on those crisp winter days. The stew would warm her down to her toes, radiating the kind of glow that only her mum's hearty food could give.

It was three o'clock in the afternoon on Thursday December 30th, 1965.

Alarm bells rang for the Walsall police who quickly identified important points that made the disappearance disturbingly comparable to that of Margaret Reynolds who had vanished three months earlier.

They identified that both girls were in the same age group and of similar height and appearance. They were snatched within a quarter of a mile from their homes and at similar times of day and both disappeared within a short distance of the A34.

As with the case of Margaret, dozens of officers were given the task of combing the area, handing out posters with her details and thoroughly searching around 2,000 homes.

As the search went on, accounts of sexual assaults and failed kidnapping appeared in the news.

Ten-year-old Patricia Kimberley reported how a man in a light blue car had stopped her in Bloxwich, and made a move to grab her. She had managed to break free and fled home to her mum.

Police remembered the assault on Julia Taylor in Leamore, Walsall, a year before but nobody was found or convicted for that attack.

Was it the same man?

Chapter 5

THE COUNTRYSIDE HAD gone into hibernation under a blanket of white. The trees glistened with frost; the air hung silent and cold. The intricate patterns of snowflakes floated weightlessly downward from the pure white sky above, each flake swirling and dancing until it reached its destined place of rest. The swirling white and the colour of the grass collided.

Breath pale against the numbing air, he blinked as the frost patiently kissed his face.

The meadows, lying peacefully in the morning light, were flattened from the hedgerows to the canopy of the woodland of Cannock Chase.

Tony Hodgkiss had been cycling across the wintry countryside on a narrow road, known as Mansty Gully, just west of the A34 a few miles north of Cannock.

Nature was calling so he decided to stop and relieve himself in a nearby field. No sooner had the bike's icy tracks been imprinted on the road; they were erased by the fresh white snow.

There was a shallow ditch at edge of the meadow. The grass was thick, growing in dense tussocks. In the ditch to one side, he saw a child's clothing.

Never before had he noticed how time was so much like water; that it can pass slowly, a drop at a time, even freeze, or rush by in a blink. Those few moments had passed like thousands of camera frames per second shown one at a time. In this slow time-bubble the coldness was colder and the silence was more silent.

He turned, but too slowly to be normal. There was sadness in his eyes. The object, he initially mistook for a doll, was the body of a little girl, lying face down in the undergrowth and shrouded by her clothing.

It was Wednesday 12th January, 1966.

Police were soon at the scene and identified the little girl as Diane Tift. She had been sexually assaulted and her attacker had evidently suffocated her by pulling the woollen pixie hood over her face and drawing its string tight around her neck.

By the time the victim was found, her flesh was as cold as the waterlogged ditch she lay in; her ivory skin splattered and her face half submerged in the gritty muck.

The killer hadn't left any evidence here. Perhaps amid all this sludge, the police could find something they needed.

Before long, a uniformed policeman noticed an object in the silt in the ditch.

In a few days the snow would have covered it again and the secrets of five months ago would have remained in their grave. But today a cyclist had stopped for a call of nature and stumbled across the gruesome scene.

The policeman's fingernails couldn't prise it free so he took a stick and started to remove the earth from round it. Then spying the tell-tale jagged lines of two fused plates he froze..

Only the crown of the skull was sticking out.

"Quick," he called out. "Come and take a look at this."

There was something in that shout, a pain behind it.

The bones of Margaret Reynolds lay almost at the same spot as the body of Diane Tift.

It was impossible to tell, after five months, how the first little girl had died but the pathologist thought that she had probably been strangled.

Chapter 6

THE BLACK COUNTRY WAS a dangerous place to be whilst a sex fiend was on the loose. The atmosphere was so brittle it could snap. Mothers started taking their children to school and returning to pick them up. No child was safe.

The two gruesome discoveries led to a large scale murder hunt led by Walsall Police and Birmingham Police, with Scotland Yard's Detective Superintendent Cyril Gold placed in charge of the investigation.

They had a sneaking suspicion that somebody was shielding the killer and continually appealed to the public for information.

Only one year before, and fifty five miles as the crow flies, is Saddleworth Moor where other children's bodies had been found, the victims of Ian Brady and Myra Hindley.

A similar monster was now at work on Cannock Chase.

The police were leafing through every statement and file. In just a few days they hoped to find the evidence, the breadcrumb trail that would lead them to the killer.

A man walked into Cannock police station. At first his eyes were cast to the floor and then he seemed to suddenly realize he was at his destination. There was a tension in his manner, tightness in his face and his eyes moved involuntarily. He pounded his knuckles so hard on the front desk that he could have bruised them.

"Good morning, sir," said the police constable. "How can I help?"

"I think I might have some information for you about those two little girls you found on the Chase," he replied.

"I see," he said, wide eyed. "And what would that be?"

"I believe that my brother is capable of murdering those girls," he replied, showing no emotion.

"What makes you so sure?" the policeman asked.

"He has sick, violent fantasies," he replied. "And he has an unnatural interest in young girls."

The policeman was quickly scribbling down what the man was telling him.

"What's your name, sir?" he asked.

"Peter Morris," he replied.

"And what's your brother's name?" he asked.

"Raymond Morris," he replied.

"And do you have an address for him?" he asked.

"Yes," he replied. "He lives at 20 Regent House, Green lane, Walsall."

"Does he live alone?" he asked.

"No, he lives with his wife, Carol," he replied.

"You do understand that this is a very serious accusation to make, don't you?" he asked. "And especially as we're talking about your brother."

The man took a step forward, now almost nose to nose with the police officer and fixed in a stare that could have frozen Loch Ness. He snarled more than spoke.

"Look," he replied. "You've been appealing to the public. I'm a member of the public and I'm here with this information, brother or not."

26

His reply took the policeman by surprise.

"And what evidence do you have to support your claim?" he asked.

"I don't have any evidence," he replied. "But I know what he's like and what he's capable of."

"Okay, sir," he said. "I'll make a report and we will look into it. Thank you."

Detectives in charge of the case investigated the claim but Morris appeared to have alibis for both murders and as a married father of two he wasn't considered to be a likely suspect for such atrocious crimes, so the report was marked 'No Further Action.'

But things were about to take a strange twist.

In October 1966, Morris was taken in by police, accused of taking two girls to his home, putting them in separate rooms and undressing them. During their questioning, neither girl was able to accurately back up the other's declaration so no charges were brought.

He'd slipped through the net again.

By summer 1967, the murder inquiry had gone cold.

Chapter 7

THE SLATE ROOFS OF the terraced houses in Camden Street, Walsall, shone like black diamonds in the August sunshine. It was the school holidays and like any other street it had become a playground for the kids who lived there.

Christine was happy with the work of art she'd created on the pavement outside her home. Even though it was only squares with numbers on, her hopscotch grid was a masterpiece for a seven year old.

There weren't many people about because most of them had gone to the Saturday market in the town centre, just a stone's throw away.

She and her playmates, eight year old Nicholas Baldry and Alwyn Isaacs had been playing hopscotch for about an hour.

"I've had enough of this, Nick," she said, "What shall we do now?"

"Let's go up there," he replied, pointing to the far end of the street.

The frayed ends of Christine's dark blue jeans were hanging over her black plimsolls as she gambolled alongside Nicholas and Alwyn, the floral print on her white T shirt glistened in the sun.

The grey car moved quietly along the street towards them, moving stealthily like a wild animal waiting to pounce on its prey.

They'd just reached Corporation Street and the driver called out to them.

"Can you tell me how I can get to Caldmore Green?" he asked.

"Yes," replied Nicholas, pointing up the street. "It's just around the corner on the right."

The man opened the passenger door.

"Maybe you can show me where it is," he said to Christine.

Her baby blue eyes lit up and the giggles rolled out of her like waves on a long, shallow beach as she jumped into the car.

Kidnapping small children was simple; he just had to pick them up and go; besides, this girl was tiny too, like a little doll. The kidnapping was over in a second. One minute she was there playing with her friends, and the next she was gone.

It was 2.20pm, Saturday 19th August, 1967.

Nicholas was troubled when he saw the car drive off in the opposite direction. Jittery and anxious, he ran back down Camden Street with Alwyn and banged loudly on the front door of Christine's house.

Mrs Lilian Darby, Christine's mum, peered at him over her horn-rimmed spectacles. Wiping her hands on her pinafore she asked,

"What's wrong, Nicholas. Why are you banging on the door?"

Taking short intakes of breath he replied, "It's Christine. She got into a man's car to show him the way to Caldmore Green but he took her a different way."

"Good Lord," she said, catching her breath in a startled grasp.

Tears blinded her as she turned, running as quickly as her legs could carry her, bolting down the street towards the off licence, her heart throbbing inside her chest with the thick grief and fear she felt as she ran.

The shop assistant jumped in fright as Mrs Darby slammed through the door.

"Quickly, quickly," she panted. "Phone the police. A man has taken Christine off in his car."

In no time the police were at the house but the kidnapper had a head start.

"Now Mrs Darby can you tell us exactly what's happened?" asked the police officer.

"Christine was out playing in the street with Nick and Alwyn," she replied, pointing to the little boys. "Not long after, Nick came running to tell me that she had got into a car. How can somebody snatch a child from the street in broad daylight?"

"So you saw what happened then?" he asked Nicholas.

"Yes," he replied.

"Can you tell me what happened then?" he asked.

"We'd been playing hopscotch," Nicholas replied. "Christine said she was fed up and wanted to do something else so we went for a walk up to the corner of the street."

"So the car was on the corner?" he asked.

"No," he replied. "We got to the corner and the car pulled up."

"What colour was the car?" he asked.

"Grey," he replied.

"Do you know what make it was?" he asked.

"It looked like that one over the road," he replied, pointing to an Austin Cambridge.

"Can you describe the man?" he asked.

"He had short, dark hair," he replied.

"What was he wearing?" he asked.

"A white shirt and a grey coat," he replied.

"And how old do you think he was?" he asked.

"I don't know" he replied. "Maybe in his thirties."

"Can you tell me what he said to you?" he asked.

"He just asked us if we could tell him where Carmer Green was," he replied. "Then he asked Christine to get in the car and show him."

"Did he ask for Carmer Green the same way as you are saying it?" he asked.

"Yes," he replied. "He spoke like I do."

"And which direction did the car go?" he asked.

"In the opposite direction," he replied. "Towards Wednesbury Road."

"Thank you, Nicholas," he said. "You've been very helpful."

The police officer realised at this point that the man was local because he pronounced Caldmore as 'Carmer.' Only a local person would pronounce it that way.

He turned to Christine's mum and said, "Don't worry, Mrs Darby. We'll have all the roads in and out of town blocked off so I'm sure we'll have Christine back with you soon."

The scream that filled the forest was like a siren. Nobody screams like that unless it is terror beyond endurance, but nobody would hear it.

He stared at her and bathed for a moment in the glory of his superiority. He'd used her for his own sexual gratification so killing her was no worse than killing an animal.

As if nothing had happened, he got back in his car, reversed down the dirt track and drove out of the forest, almost knocking down a woman who was walking her dog.

Bathed in their own putrid fumes, lorries sped past him as he drove south along the A34 towards Walsall.

A mother and her three daughters strolled by the hedgerows and two little boys stood watching the slow-moving progress of a combine harvester.

The road curved past the gauntness of Littleton Colliery and its man-made conical slag heap.

The open countryside was now a long way behind him as he crossed the Walsall boundary with the grey blocks of redevelopment flats ahead of him. He knew, as he passed through Bloxwich town centre, that he wasn't far from home.

He pulled the car up on the parking area in front of the multi-storey block of flats and got out. He turned and glanced across at Walsall police headquarters just across the street. His face was one of barely concealed glee, there was accomplishment in his eyes and his mouth twitched upwards on the left, dimpling his cheek. He casually walked into the building.

The lift was a small, creaky thing that moved with a judder and smelled of urine. When it reached the fourth floor, the doors opened with a 'ding'.

"Hello, darling," he said, entering the flat.

"Don't you darling me," she said, slamming her fist down onto the table so hard the dishes jumped. "You're late."

"My boss asked me to stay behind" he said, trying to calm her down. "He wanted to know what had been going on at the factory while he was away on holiday."

"Well," she replied. "You'll have to wait for your dinner because we have to go into town before the shops close. My mother forgot to buy some cakes while we were out shopping this morning. If we hurry, we'll be in time to get them. We can eat when we get back."

"Okay," he said.

The town centre was a river of people, their vibrant clothes shining in the afternoon sun. Everyone was moving in different directions. There was chatter between sellers and buyers. It was busy, but the hustle and bustle brought life to the town. It was market day so there were always more people about, especially as it was a lovely August afternoon.

Carol went into Marks and Spencer and picked up the cakes for her mother.

When at last they arrived, her mother was chatting to a neighbour on the front step.

"Here are you cakes, mum," she said, handing them to her.

"Come on inside," her mother said," How much do I owe you?"

"Nothing," she replied. "It's my treat."

They went into the living room where Carol's father was watching the football pools results on TV."

"It looks as if I have to carry on working," he said, shaking his head. "We haven't won the pools this week."

"Why are all those police in the town centre?" asked Carol.

"A little girl has gone missing," her mother replied.

"There was a newsflash on the telly just before they gave the pools results," her father said. "Police say a local man took her off in his car."

"How do they know he's local?" Morris asked.

"The young lad who was with her at the time said he spoke with a local accent," he replied. "They're saying that it could be the same bloke that killed those other two kids, you know, the ones they found on Cannock Chase last year."

"Well if it's the same bloke," said Morris. "He's too clever for the police. They'll never catch him, even if he's right under their noses."

Chapter 8

BY THE NEXT MORNING, Sunday, an extensive search was in progress made up of police on foot, police on horseback, and the army. The fact of the matter was that in an area the size of Cannock Chase, it was like looking for a needle in a haystack.

Six officers of the Staffordshire forces section were riding in an extended line eastwards from the A34.

One of the officers, Police Constable Arthur Ellis, had been riding his horse about half a mile when he saw what looked like a piece of cloth hanging on the branch of a fallen tree. He got down from his horse, picked the cloth off the branch and found that it was a pair of child's faeces stained knickers.

They were taken to Christine's home where her grandmother positively identified them as belonging to the girl. She recognised her own stitching in a repair she had made.

Hopes of finding Christine alive were dashed.

It was now Monday and still no sign of Christine.

A forestry worker wandered through the forest, only hearing his feet tread, hearing the cracking twigs and leaves underfoot. He had no idea of what was ahead. He kept moving forward....then he saw it. A small dark shaped object in the bracken. He picked it up. It was a child's plimsoll. It lay in the bracken a few yards into the trees and looked as if someone had thrown it from a passing car. It wasn't far from the spot where police recovered her underwear the day before.

Christine's panic-stricken grandmother identified it as one she had been wearing on the day she went missing.

Two days after the disappearance of Christine, Camden Street wasn't the same. The silence surrounded the area like a fresh, pure, white blanket of snow on a winter's day. No children were playing there even though the school holidays were at their peak. The fear had bitten deep. Those who were about gripped the hands of parents, and in other parts of the area, children were playing in their back yards. Worried parents were now keeping an even closer watch than usual on them.

Extensive house to house inquiries were going on in Walsall and posters of Christine had been posted throughout the Midlands.

Police were now linking her disappearance with the murders of Margaret Reynolds and Diane Tift which had happened eighteen months previously:

- All three girls looked similar in appearance.
- They were in the same age group and all lived near the A34.
- They all vanished near their homes.

As fears grew for Christine's safety, police believed that someone was deliberately concealing a man's identity.

Phone calls were coming in to Walsall police station with people saying that they had seen a man with a little girl fitting Christine's description, driving a grey car on Cannock Chase on the same afternoon she disappeared.

The first place to be checked was Mansty Gully and police were keeping it under surveillance. However, after receiving this information they cordoned off the area and concentrated the search on where people had seen the car.

By eight o'clock on Tuesday morning, the search teams were ready to start again.

The long, drawn out line moved slowly forward, heads down, sticks prodding the ground as they moved on and on further into the woods.

The forest that stood before him was eerie. The sky had vanished almost completely, only a few fragments of blue remained like scattered pieces of a difficult jigsaw puzzle. The only movement was the occasional bird, startling in a tree, or a squirrel dashing up a nearby trunk.

A path had been trodden through the waist high bracken, not wide, just enough to show a person had entered. The soldier, Private Michael Blundred, followed the path of broken stems to what at first glance was a bundle of clothes. He took his stick and gave it a gentle prod. In a flash the bundle took on the appearance of a child. He came to a halt. Tears ran down his face as he looked away. He raised his hand and called out, "I've found her. She's over here."

The sprawled body of seven-year-old Christine Darby was lying in a furrow beneath brushwood at the foot of a tree only a mile away from where Margaret Reynolds and Diane Tift were discovered.

Her arms were spread outwards, her legs were apart with her knees raised, and she was naked from the waist down, apart from her clean white socks which indicated that she had been carried there. Her jeans were a few feet away. Her genital area had been severely torn in the vicious sexual attack.

The search for Christine had come to an end, seventy two hours after she had gone missing.

Now it seemed the same man had reappeared and that a new series of killings had begun.

It was 22nd August 1967.

Chapter 9

LORRAINE AND WENDY Elsmore were playing outside their parents' fish and chip shop with their friend, Elaine Bailey. Lorraine began to think about how they could sneak away and make their way to a nearby field and play there instead.

The people standing behind each other like a flock of sheep, all wanting to get a bite of the delicious fish and chips which anyone could smell from a mile away, were getting on her nerves.

She watched, and her insides curdled like milk with lemon juice, as a woman left the chippy and shoved a handful of chips into her mouth, making a contented noise at the back of her throat.

"That's it," she thought. "Come on Wendy. Come on Elaine, let's go round the block and play in the field."

On that sultry day in mid-August the pond looked like a mirror. From the tall pines around the edge came not a sound, no movement of branches, no birds calling.

"Let's go and play by the pool," she said. "We might be lucky and find some frogs."

Their giggles wended their way through the long grass as the three girls waded through it. They wanted to make the most of the furnace summer that had turned Cannock Chase bone dry.

"If ever mom finds out we've been here," said Wendy. "She's going to go mad. She's warned us not to play here."

Their mum was very strict. The thought of a monster on the loose terrified her. She dreaded to think that her kids could be dragged off to some unknown, godforsaken place to be assaulted and murdered.

A sadistic reign of terror cast its shadow over Cannock and the surrounding area. However, children had been placed on guard by the warning posters scattered around the district.

They were looking in the pool to see if they could see any frogs when the sound of breaking twigs made them turn around.

The man beckoned to them.

Lorraine drew her eight-year-old sister to her side.

Elaine's little face slackened; her brow furrowed - eyes darting about in concern as if she were searching for a place to hide.

"Do you want to come with me?" he asked.

"No," Lorraine replied.

"You've got to come with me because your mum has sent me to pick you up," he said. "She wants you home straight away and she's sent me to take you back."

Their mother couldn't have sent the stranger because she was unaware of their whereabouts so Lorraine knew the man was lying.

"We don't know you," she said. "And my mom has warned us not to speak to strangers."

Inside, he could feel his heart beating more quickly. His hands started shaking. He knew he had failed this time. Biting his upper lip, he turned around and walked off towards the white van which was parked in the lane.

Once he had driven off, the children ran home.

Chapter 10

THE MISSING CHILD CASE had now turned into one of murder and Scotland Yard's Detective Chief Superintendent Ian Forbes was assigned the case.

The pathologist determined that Christine wasn't killed at the scene where her body was found. Although her plimsolls were missing, the soles of her white socks were clean, which implied that she had been carried dead or unconscious to where she was found.

All three murder victims - Margaret, Diane, and Christine - lived near the A34, within 17 miles of each other. Cannock Chase is on the A34. Increasingly this geographical link became significant in the investigation.

The kidnapper picked the three girls up in the afternoon. The only difference was that Margaret and Diane were by themselves when they were abducted, but Christine was with her friends.

It was just a matter of time before the murder mystery that shocked millions ended most surprisingly.

The young boy, who originally recalled Morris' accent when he asked for directions to 'Carmer Green', led officers to concentrate the hunt within the Walsall area.

There was no technology, DNA or that kind of stuff to help police at that time, which made the investigation prolonged. Everything was done manually by detectives having to painstakingly search through piles of paperwork.

Raymond Morris was already a suspect but at that stage, he was one of many. Now the pieces of the jigsaw puzzle were beginning to slot together.

He had made his big mistake when he tried to abduct Margaret Aulton on the eve of Bonfire night.

Mrs Lane had memorised his number plate and the police were now checking it.

Detective Constable Conrad Joseph and his colleague Detective Constable Atkins woke the local Vehicle Tax Officer to access the vehicle records at the Walsall office.

The registration given by Mrs Lane was 429 LOP but this wasn't registered to a green and white Ford Corsair.

Instead of giving up, they worked into the night meticulously searching through documents, one by one, for similar registration numbers. Rearranging the numbers 29 to 92 they discovered that 492 LOP was a matching vehicle and owned by Raymond Morris.

The next morning they made their way to Oldbury to the factory where he worked and he was called into a private office.

"Good morning, Mr. Morris," said Detective Constable Joseph. "This is my colleague, Detective Constable Atkins. We'd like to invite you into the police station for a chat to assist us with our enquiries. I can assure you that you will be free to leave at any time and there's nothing to worry about."

"That's okay," he said. "I'll do anything I can to help. This won't be the first time the police have interviewed me. In fact, I'm getting used to it."

Chatting on the way to the police station, he mentioned he used to own an Austin A55. An Austin A55 was the type of vehicle linked to Christine's murder.

The harsh artificial light flooded the room as he took a chair. It looked more like a prison cell than an interview room. Two more detectives entered.

"Hello, Mr Morris," said Detective Constable James Speight. "You've met Detective Constables Atkins and Joseph. This is my colleague Detective Sergeant Farrell. We've brought you here to help with our enquiries. You do not have to say anything but it may harm your defence if you do not mention when questioned something which you later rely on in court. Anything you do say may be given in evidence. Speaking to us is voluntary and as such, you may remain silent or answer no comment if you wish. You are entitled to have a solicitor with you but finding one will take some time. Do you understand?"

"Yes," he replied.

"Would you like a solicitor to be present?" he asked.

"No," he replied.

"The interview will be recorded," he said, switching on the tape. "What is your full name?"

Morris's eyes focussed on some invisible apparition, his eyelids a little slow to blink, his pupils at a standstill. It was as if his brain was suffering a short circuit and was struggling to process the question.

"Raymond Leslie Morris," he answered.

"And what is your date of birth?" he asked.

"The thirteenth of August, 1929," he replied.

"What is your marital status?" he asked.

"I'm married," he replied.

"And what's your address?" he asked.

"I live across the street at 20 Regents House, Green Lane, Walsall," he replied.

"Could you tell me what you were doing between six o'clock and nine o' clock on Tuesday evening November the fourth?" he asked.

"I was at home with my wife," he replied.

"Can your wife confirm this?" he asked.

"Yes," he replied.

"The reason you're here, Mr Morris," he said. "Is that someone took the registration number of your car. Apparently it was seen in the area where an attempted abduction of a young girl happened."

"I told you I was at home with my wife," he said, staring at the detective.

"Then you won't mind taking part in an identity parade, will you?" he asked.

"Not at all," he replied.

"I'll take you to another part of the building where we'll take your fingerprints and a couple of photos," he said. "Then you'll stand in line with another four men similar to yourself."

With hands clasped tightly in front of her stomach she constantly fiddled with her knuckles, weaving her fingers in and out of each other.

The police officer laid his hand lightly on Mrs. Lane's shoulder.

"It's okay, Mrs. Lane," he said "You just have to walk past the line of men. If you recognise the man you saw attacking the little girl you just tell me which one it is."

She slowly walked up and down the line looking at each man carefully. After a moment she looked at the police officer and shook her head.

"I can't see him there," she said.

Morris was allowed to walk away free.

Chapter 11

SOMETHING ABOUT RAYMOND Leslie Morris left detectives Joseph and Atkins feeling uneasy. Remaining convinced of his guilt they sought permission from Detective Chief Inspector George Read to stay on the case. He agreed so they started delving into Morris's past. They knew he had been questioned over the Christine Darby murder, but was given an alibi by his wife, effectively putting him out of the inquiry. It was Morris' admission to them that he had previously owned an Austin A55 – the type previously linked to Christine's murder – that niggled away at them. And the pair began to wonder what vehicle he had driven before the period 1965-68, when he was known to have the Austin. Specifically, they wanted to find out what he was driving in December, 1964, when an eight-year-old girl was abducted in Leamore, Walsall.

DC Joseph went to the engineering firm where Morris had worked in 1964. The workmen could not remember the registration of the car he drove at the time, but they remembered it as being large and flashy.

It was a two-tone blue Vauxhall Velox Car, which had a spot light fitted to the driver's door pillar.

DC Joseph said: "Did you know that the young man who found Julia Taylor saw a large Vauxhall car driving away from the scene in Bloxwich Lane at about 9.45pm shortly before investigating her muffled cry from the waste ground where she was found?"

"Yes," DC Atkins replied. "But he didn't take the car registration number or the model."

"I know," he said. "But he said that it had a spot lamp fixed to the door pillar. We'll have to check with Morris's car insurance company and see if they have details of his previously insured cars. I'll contact the officer in charge of Oldbury CID and ask if they can arrange for him to be stopped by police on his way to work. They can ask him to show them his insurance documents."

The stop was made and, armed with details of his insurer, the detectives managed to track down his Walsall-based broker.

The office manager's silver flecked hair had a military look about it but the skin on his chin was as smooth as a baby's bottom.

"Good morning, sir," said DC Joseph. "I'm Detective Constable Joseph and this is my colleague Detective Constable Atkins. If you remember, I spoke to you on the phone yesterday afternoon asking if we could come and check the records of Mr Raymond Morris."

His cheeks dimpled, and the corner of his eyes wrinkled.

"That's right," he said. "I have them here ready for you."

As he talked, he straightened the stuff on his desk, making sure everything was organised. There wasn't much: a phone, a legal-sized lined white pad, a transparent Bic pen with a black top, and a big plastic frame with pictures of his wife, his children and a cocker spaniel.

"I'll leave you alone so you can check through them," he said, and left the office.

"Look at this, Conrad," said DC Atkins. "He insured a two-tone Vauxhall Velox between November 1962and November 1965, registration number VTB 625."

"And here's another, Ted," said DC Joseph. "He also insured a grey, Austin Grampian and he had that car at the time of Christine Darby's abduction."

"It looks like we've got him," said DC Atkins.

"Not yet," DC Joseph said. "I want to investigate more."

"We don't need more, do we?" DC Atkins asked.

"I want to see what other cars he's owned," he replied. "I want to see if he had access to any other cars. I suspect he might have had a company car. I'll contact the Income Tax Office in Dudley when we get back to the station."

He contacted the office and they told him that at the time of the abductions and murders of Carol Stephens, Margaret Reynolds, and Diane Tift, Morris had been working for a toiletries and cleaning firm based in Sheffield.

"Right," he said, picking up the phone. "I'm going to call the CID in Sheffield and ask them to visit the firm and get hold of his employment details, what his areas of responsibility were and what vehicles they provided."

When the telephone conversation ended, he sat back in his chair thinking what to do next.

"So what's going to happen now?" DC Atkins asked.

"Not a lot," he replied. "They said they'd go to the company tomorrow morning and I should get the details tomorrow afternoon."

"Why don't you ring Cannock Police Station and ask them if they have any more info on him?" he asked.

"It's a waste of time with them," he replied. "Every time I speak to them I get the same response. Not one officer in Cannock is interested in our inquiry. I was told on several occasions that his wife had given him an alibi. The last time I phoned them the officer had the nerve to ask me how many more times I was going to pester them. He said he'd been eliminated and that was that."

"Well we've been working on this report for five days now so another day won't matter," said DC Atkins.

Minutes changed to hours as he sat motionlessly. Twenty four hours passed in the blink of an eye, before they got the results they had been waiting for.

DC Joseph tingled from his head to his toes. He bounced on his flexing feet and rubbed his hands together. He felt like every fibre of his being was vibrating with anticipation. His hands trembled and his eyes were wide.

"This is what a cat must feel like waiting to pounce on a mouse," he thought.

"It looks like you have some good news," DC Atkins said.

"At last, Ted," he said, waving the document. "It's all here. Morris worked as a sales representative from his home across the street and was responsible for covering Birmingham, Staffordshire, Shropshire, Worcestershire, and South Wales. His clients were mainly hospitals and factories. Here, come and have a look."

DC Atkin's brain tingled like a hand that's been sat on for too long. A smirk was playing at the corner of his lips as he sat staring at the document.

"I see he was provided with a green coloured Hillman Super Minx Estate car that was authorised for his own use as well," he said.

"And look at these mileage returns," DC Joseph said. "He was in Aston on September 8, 1965, the day that Margaret Reynolds disappeared."

"And he disclosed private use in the Cannock and Great Wyrley areas when Diane was taken," said DC Atkins. "It seems he was in the right place, at the right time, in the right kind of car."

"I'm handing over our report with this information to Detective Superintendent Ian Forbes." said DC Joseph. "Let's see what he thinks of it."

An hour and a half later Mr Forbes returned.

"Go and arrest him," he said.

Chapter 12

THE ENGINE COUGHED as he turned the key. His breath lingered in the air for a moment before disappearing completely. His gloved hands banged on the steering wheel. He pulled the choke out slightly and turned the key again. The tension that had started to build up inside him melted into nothing. The engine started.

He had just pulled out onto Green Lane when he was stopped by a police Panda car.

The policeman spoke into his personal radio and advised the detectives across the street at the West Midlands Police Headquarters that he'd stopped the suspect.

"Good morning sir," the police officer said. "Could I see your driving license?"

Before the man could answer, two detectives had arrived.

"Thank you," one of the detectives said to the police officer, as he took his place by the car door.

Without warning he swooped into the car, like an eagle after its prey, and snatched the keys out of the ignition switch. He took a strong grip on the suspect's right shoulder.

"I'm Detective Chief Inspector Molloy from Cannock CID," he said in a severe manner. "I am detaining you in connection with the murder of Christine Darby at Cannock Chase on the 19th of August, 1967. You are not obliged to say anything unless you wish to do so, but whatever you say will be taken down in writing and may be given in evidence."

In that instant Morris's skin became greyed, his mouth hung with lips slightly parted and his eyes were as wide as they could stretch.

"Oh God. Is it my wife?" he mumbled, sitting there petrified at the sound of the detective's voice

"Get out of this bloody car," Molloy said.

He sat there motionless.

"Get out," he said again. "Do as I tell you. If you don't get out I'll yank you out."

He still didn't move.

He gasped as he felt the firm grip of Molloy's hands on his shoulders hauling him out of the car. The other detective quickly took hold of his right arm. They walked him across the street, which was now blocked with traffic, to their parked car.

Detective Molloy drove while another two detectives sat in the back with Morris. It moved like a bullet up the M6 motorway towards its destination. Nobody attempted to say a word during the journey.

The Station Sergeant stepped back as the swing doors almost flew from their hinges. Molloy thrust the man to the counter.

"I've arrested this man for the murder of Christine Darby," he said. "His name is Raymond Leslie Morris. Put him on a charge sheet and I'll put him in a cell. Mr. Forbes and Mr. Bailey are going to interview him later this morning."

All the details were taken down and they put him in a cell. Molloy removed the man's personal belongings, as well as his belt and shoelaces, just in case he tried to harm himself. He slammed the door and handed the belongings to the sergeant.

He appeared to be tall as he entered the cell but when he got closer to Morris, he could see that he was an average five foot something. He appeared taller because he had got a menacing look about him, the kind of look that makes someone feel insignificant with just a twitch of his eyebrow. His stocky frame was hidden beneath his middle class average suit.

"My name is Forbes," he said, in his broad Scottish accent. "Detective Chief Superintendent Ian Forbes. Do you know who I am?"

"Yes," Morris replied.

"You will be held here for now. We have several other enquiries to make."

Morris slumped in the chair and waited a few seconds before shrugging and nodding his head.

Mr. Forbes had already given instructions for the man's wife to be taken to a separate police station for interview.

After lunch, Mr. Forbes and Detective Chief Inspector Molloy arrived at Hednesford Police Station.

The twenty five year old woman, waiting for them, could have graced any magazine cover. She had only been married to the accused man for four years and she was his second wife.

"Good afternoon, Mrs Morris," said Mr Forbes quietly. "I know this is going to be difficult for you to take in but your husband is the Cannock Chase murderer."

There was shyness to her, hesitation in her body movements and softness in her voice

"He can't be," she said, lips trembling.

"Could you have been mistaken about him going shopping with you on August 19th?" he asked.

"No," she replied. "We went to get some cakes my mum had forgotten."

"Do you think that the passing of time has played tricks with your memory?" he asked. "It's now the fifteenth of November."

"I know exactly where we were that day," she replied.

The questioning went on for about three quarters of an hour but nothing worked.

"I'm just going to check on something with the desk sergeant," Mr. Forbes said, looking at Detective Inspector Molloy. "I'll be back shortly."

He left the room.

Detective Molloy leaned forward. Looking into her eyes he said quietly, "You know, you can forget your husband. My presumption is that you'll never see him again. We say he's the Cannock Chase murderer, so the way things are going he's had it. He's finished. He's a child killer, just like Ian Brady. The only thing left for us to decide is whether or not you are another Myra Hindley."

She looked at him as if he'd grown another head.

"Huh?" she asked.

He stared back at her as though she was from another planet.

"You know who Myra Hindley is, don't you?"

She shook her head.

"You don't?" he asked.

She shook her head again.

"Have you never heard about the Moors Murders?" he asked.

"Yes," she replied. "I've heard about them."

"Well," he said. "Myra Hindley stood and laughed as she watched her boyfriend rape and strangle a ten year old little girl. They even tape recorded her being tortured."

Her silent weeping was worse than if she had screamed. He wanted to comfort her until she felt safe enough to cry out loud. But he was a tough detective and immune to the weeping of a young woman.

For twenty minutes he went into detail about the poor child's suffering at the hands of the killers while she sat sobbing quietly.

"Well," he whispered, putting his hand on her shoulder. "Are you another Myra Hindley?"

"No," she sobbed. "I'm not."

"Your husband didn't get home from work at the time you said, did he?"

She raised her head and looked up at him, the tears running down her face.

"No. He was late," she replied. "He told me his boss had kept him behind at work. I was annoyed because we had to hurry to the shops before they closed to get some cakes for my mother."

"So what you told the police was a lie?" he asked.

"What's your name?" she asked.

"Detective Chief Inspector Pat Molloy," he replied.

After all what she had gone through, the pain ebbed.

"I didn't lie, honestly," she said. "He told the police he was with me and I just agreed with him when they asked me if it was true. I didn't think it mattered. I didn't think he could be connected with anything like that."

She put her face into her hands.

"Do you want to make another statement telling us what really happened that day?" he asked.

She looked up at him again.

"Yes," she replied. "Do you think I could have a cigarette?"

"Of course," he replied. "I'll go and get one for you."

As he was going down the passageway, he bumped into Ian Forbes who was making his way back to interview her.

"Whatever you do," he said to Mr. Forbes. "Don't go in there yet. She's going to make another statement. She's busted his alibi and wants a cigarette."

He quickly returned with them and he and Mr. Forbes entered the room.

"How are you now, my dear?" Mr. Forbes asked, sitting next to her.

"I'm all right, thank you," she replied, gripping her cigarette.

"Now," he said. "Could you tell us exactly what happened that day?"

"I told the police that my husband had arrived home at about two o' clock," she replied. "Now I come to think of it this could not have been so, but I wasn't telling lies. I remember clearly that my mother had asked me to get her some cakes from Marks and Spencer in Walsall. She had forgotten to get them while we were out shopping that morning. As soon as my husband returned home from work, we went out almost immediately into town to get the cakes as the shops were about to close."

"Go on," he said.

"I remember that as we drove through Walsall, the police were stopping cars and speaking to the drivers. This must have been between five and six o'clock," she said. "I honestly believed that what I told the police was true because I trusted him implicitly."

"Thank you, Mrs. Morris," he said. "That will be all for the moment. You've been very helpful."

"Can I go now?" she asked.

"Yes," he replied.

"Will I have to be a witness?" she asked.

"We can ask you to give evidence," he replied. "But by British law we cannot force a wife to give evidence against her husband. That choice will be yours if you are asked."

After she had left, Mr. Forbes and Mr. Molloy immediately sent Detective Norman Williams to see her parents to establish what time the Morris's had arrived at their home that day.

Chapter 13

THE HOUSE WAS IDENTICAL to the neighbouring ones right down to the shade of paint on the doors and window frames. He checked the number on the door and wrapped the brass knocker three times and waited. The door opened a little and a petite woman looked out.

"Good evening," he said. "Are you Mrs. Horsley?"

"Yes," she replied. "Can I help you?"

"I'm Norman Williams from the Cannock Chase murder squad," he replied. "Could I come in and have a word with you and your husband?"

She poked her head out of the door and looked up and down the street.

"It's okay," he said, pointing to a parked car. "That's my car there. I haven't come in a police car so you needn't worry about what your neighbours might think."

"Please come in," she said and led him into the living room.

"This is Mr. Williams from the police," she said, turning to her husband.

His hand gripped the hand of Mr. Williams like a vice. "Pleased to meet you," he said.

"I'd like to ask you a few questions regarding your son in law," he said.

"Oh, do sit down," said Mrs. Horsley. "Would you like something to drink?"

"No, thank you," he replied. "I won't be taking up too much of your time."

"So," said Mr. Horsley. "What's Ray been up to that brings you here?"

"I hate to have to tell you this," he replied. "But we have reason to believe that your son in law is the Cannock Chase murderer."

Mrs. Horsley gasped, quickly placing her hand across her mouth.

"Chief Superintendent Forbes and Detective Inspector Molloy have interviewed your daughter, Carol, and I just want to hear your version of what time they arrived here on Saturday the 19th of August."

"I remember being in something of a panic about some cakes I'd forgotten to buy when I was out shopping with Carol that morning," Mrs. Horsley said. "Carol said she'd get them for me when Ray came home from work. I was watching the clock anxiously as the time drew near for Marks and Spencer to close. They got here about five o' clock. He said he'd got home from work late because his boss had been on holiday and he'd stayed behind to give him details of what had gone on while he'd been away."

"It was after five," said Mr. Horsley. "I remember that because it was sometime after the football results."

"That's right," she said. "I remember you saying you hadn't been lucky enough to win them."

"They didn't stay long," he said. "They left the cakes and went back to their flat because Carol had left a steak in the oven."

"They returned later in the evening at about eight," said Mrs. Horsley. "The four of us went out for a drink at a pub in Stone."

"That's a bit of a way to go for a drink," said Mr. Williams, raising his eyebrows.

"Ray said he fancied a drive out into the country," said Mr. Horsley.

"You'd have to drive past Cannock Chase to get to Stone from here, wouldn't you?" he asked.

"I remember us driving past the Chase," she replied. "I remember making a remark about the missing girl and the possibility that her body might end up there. Ray commented that the police would never catch the killer because he was too clever for them."

Meanwhile, back at Stafford Police Station, Ian Forbes was interviewing Raymond Morris again.

"I have to caution you that you are not obliged to answer any questions I ask unless you wish to do so. Anything you do say will be taken down and may be used in evidence," he said. "You have been held here in connection with the murder of Christine Darby. Do you wish to say anything to me about it?"

He scanned the prisoner's face for a reaction and the silence hung in the air like the suspended moment before a falling glass shatters on the floor.

"Do you wish to say anything to me about it?" he asked again, with the same result. "Do you admit or deny being responsible?"

There was another long silence. Morris's face was haggard. His eyes had a distant faraway look, like a sailor staring out to sea.

"Whatever I say will make no difference," he replied.

"What do you mean by that?" asked Mr. Forbes.

"I'm finished," he replied.

"I don't know what you mean," said Mr. Forbes.

"It doesn't make any difference now," he said.

"I'm finding it very difficult to understand what you are trying to say," said Mr. Forbes.

There was another long silence.

Mr. Forbes's eyebrows furrowed as he leaned forward.

"Are you feeling all right?" he asked. "Do you understand what I'm saying to you and the situation you are in?"

He nodded but didn't answer.

"Are you still saying that you arrived home at two o' clock that Saturday?" he asked.

"What's the point of all this?" Morris asked.

"You are in a very serious situation," Mr. Forbes said. "Would you like a glass of water or a cup of tea?"

"No," he replied. "I told you I got home at my usual time. I went shopping that afternoon with my wife. Why don't you ask her?"

"You are not telling me the truth," he said. "I've interviewed your wife and she told me that you didn't arrive home that afternoon until four thirty."

His heart sank into his shoes. No thoughts came to him except that his fate was sealed. Shaking his head and putting it into his hands, he muttered, "Oh God. Oh God. She wouldn't. She wouldn't."

There was a knock on the door, and Norman Williams handed the statements from the prisoner's in-laws to Mr. Forbes.

"I'll ask you again," he said. "Did you return home at your normal time on Saturday the 19th of August?"

There was another period of silence.

Shaking the papers at him, Mr. Forbes asked, "Do you know what I have here?"

No answer.

"I'll ask you for the last time. Did you arrive home at your usual time on Saturday the 19th of August?"

There was still no answer.

"Okay," Mr. Forbes said. "I'll tell you what I have here. These statements were made by your wife's mother and father. They say that you and your wife arrived at her house in Beddows Road around five o'clock that afternoon. Your mother-in-law says you told her you had only just got home from work. What have you got to say about that?"

Chapter 14

THE POLICE HAD RECEIVED statements from two different people who claim to have been on Cannock Chase on the day Christine Darby went missing. They told them they had seen a man in a grey car very close to where her body was found.

Ian Forbes insisted on putting Raymond Morris on an identification parade but he refused. So another plan had to be thought of to charge the culprit with murder.

He had already been in custody for over twenty four hours. The police needed a positive identification before any charge could be made or they would have to let him go.

"Pat," he said to Detective Molloy. "Can you drive to Victor Whitehouse's home and bring him back here? Morris won't go on an identification parade and I can't force him. Not to worry though, I have an idea."

"And what would that be, sir?" he asked.

"Once Mr. Whitehouse is here," he replied. "You can take Morris outside into the exercise yard and I'll come out with Mr. Whitehouse and bring him face to face with him. He said he'd recognise the man again if he saw him. This is our only chance."

Detective Molloy got into his car and sped off to Hednesford. When he arrived, Mr. Whitehouse wasn't at home. It was still early morning and he'd gone for a walk on Cannock Chase.

Detective Molloy wasn't going to give up. He drove to the Chase to look for him, even though he knew it was going to be like looking for a needle in a haystack.

It was going to be his lucky day. Although he had never met Mr. Whitehouse, when he got to the forest, he saw a man approaching him. He was a clear head high than most people. Detective Molloy wondered how many comments he got daily about his stature and the jibes he would get about 'the air being cold up there.'

The man's legs moved slowly as each stride brought him closer to Detective Molloy.

"Excuse me," said Molloy. "Would you happen to be Victor Whitehouse?"

"Yes," he replied.

Detective Molloy was gobsmacked. He'd found the needle in the haystack.

Shaking his hand he said, "I'm Detective Chief Inspector Molloy. I don't know if you've heard but we've arrested a man who we think murdered Christine Darby."

"I have," he said.

"I've been sent to pick you up and take you to Stafford Police Station. Detective Chief Superintendent Forbes would like to see you. He wants to see if the man you saw by the car in the forest here on the day of the murder is the same man we have in custody."

His cheeks dimpled, and the corner of his eyes wrinkled.

"Definitely," he said. "How are we going to get there?"

"My car's just over there," he replied, pointing through the trees. "We'll be there in no time," he replied.

When they arrived at the police station, Detective Molloy, Chief Superintendent Forbes, and two other detectives went to the prisoner's cell.

"You remember last night I told you I planned to put you on an identification parade and you refused?" Forbes asked. "Have you thought any more about it?"

"No way will I go on parade," he replied, without hesitation.

Mr. Forbes looked at Detective Molloy. "Take him out," he said.

He took Morris by the arm and led him out into an enclosed space, open to the sky but covered with bars to prevent escape. He took him to the far end and stood him against the wall as if placing a prisoner to face a firing squad.

Morris stood there waiting.

A few seconds later, Ian Forbes appeared from the building with Victor Whitehouse.

Mr. Whitehouse walked across the yard and stood face to face with Morris.

"Have you seen this man before?" asked Forbes

Mr. Whitehouse stared at Morris, not taking his eyes off him. He thought long and hard. Turning to Mr. Forbes he replied, "Yes. I'd say yes."

Detective Molloy took Morris, who showed no emotion, back to his cell, while Mr. Whitehouse went to make a written statement about the identification.

The detectives now had sufficient evidence to charge Morris with Christine Darby's murder.

News travels fast. By the time the police convoy arrived at Cannock Police Station, there was a sizeable crowd of people waiting outside. The detectives took Morris in through the back door, his head covered by a blanket.

"Raymond Leslie Morris," Mr. Forbes said. "I charge you with the murder of Christine Anne Darby on or about the 19th of August, 1967, in the County of Stafford, contrary to the Common Law. You need not say anything if you don't wish but anything you do say will be taken down and may be used in evidence."

Looking as if he'd given up all hope he answered, "Can you arrange a solicitor?"

He appeared before a specially convened magistrates' court who remanded him in custody until the date of his trial was set.

The detectives went to a nearby pub to celebrate.

A young, uniformed police officer came into the pub and made his way to Detective Molloy.

"Excuse me sir," he said, handing a small brown envelope to him. "The prison officers in reception found this round Morris's ankle when they searched him."

He opened the envelope and pulled out a man's wrist-watch with a metal expanding bracelet.

"Around his ankle?" he asked.

"Yes sir, his ankle," he replied. "I can't think why he was wearing it around his ankle. Does it mean anything to you?"

"Not a thing," he replied.

Not long after, another police officer came into the pub and made a bee line for Detective Molloy.

"Excuse me, sir," he said. "Could you come to the station with me and have a look at something interesting we've found?"

He returned with him to the police station. The police officer handed him a Kodak photographic paper box.

"We found this in the spare bedroom at Morris's flat," he said. "It was sealed and it says only to be opened in a darkened room. Look what we found inside."

He handed nine black and white photos to Molloy.

His eyes opened wide as he saw photos of a little girl in various stages of undress. One of them showed a close up of a man's penis near the child's private parts. The child's face could be seen but he could only see the man's trousers and his hands.

Molloy reached into his pocket and pulled out the wrist-watch that prison officer's had found on Morris's ankle.

On the wrist of hands of the man interfering with the little girl in the photos was the same wrist-watch that Molloy had just pulled out of his pocket.

"But who is the little girl in the photos?" he asked. "And where was his wife when he was taking them?"

The only answer to that, of course, was to pay another visit to Carol Morris.

He went to see her at her parents' home because she had moved out of the flat.

"Ah, Mrs Morris," he said. "I have some photographs here I'd like to show you. You might find them a bit disturbing but we need to know if you can identify the little girl in them."

She felt like burping up and being sick right there.

"It's my niece," she replied.

"And could I ask you where you were when your husband was taking these photos?" he asked.

"I would have been in the other room," she replied. "Where did you find them?"

"My men found them when they gave your flat a good turnover," he replied. "They were in a box which said could only be opened in a dark room so if you ever saw it you wouldn't have thought any more of it."

"I can't believe he could have done such things under my very nose," she said.

"This will also be used in evidence against him," he said. "So far we have him on a murder charge, attempting to abduct a child, and now this."

"I want nothing more to do with him," she said, removing her wedding ring.

Chapter 15

BUILT OF GREY STONE, thick walls, with bars on the unpleasant windows, the courthouse smelled of centuries of fear. This was the Shire Hall, Stafford, where the trial of Raymond Leslie Morris would begin.

Snowflakes swirled and danced in the ice cold wind outside whilst the group of people waiting to get a place inside looked more like a crowd waiting for a new year sale.

It was the 10th of February, 1969.

The jury, made up of nine men and three women, had been called and the court was listening to the opening speech.

The cold, fixed stare never wavered as child killer Raymond Morris listened to the chilling warning that raised the curtain on his Staffordshire Assizes trial.

"This was a hateful crime of lust and you will shortly have to look at some unpleasant photographs," the Judge, Mr. Justice Ashworth told jurors.

Morris betrayed not one sliver of emotion as the judge added, "But you are here to judge calmly, dispassionately now whether it can be proved that it is the accused man, Raymond Leslie Morris, who is guilty."

Those in the court, those who followed the case through newspaper accounts were far from calm or dispassionate. Three years earlier they had struggled to grasp the barbarity behind the Moors Murders. Standing before them on that cold day was a new demon. They had gathered in the gallery and queued outside the imposing building to see harsh justice done.

Morris had denied Christine Darby's murder and the attempted abduction of Margaret Aulton. He admitted the indecent assault of a five-year-old girl.

The first witness to be called was Nicholas Baldry, Christine's playmate, and now nine years old.

"Can you tell the court what happened when you and Christine were playing the day she went missing?" Mr. Brian Gibbens, QC, prosecuting asked.

"Christine, me, and our friend were walking up Camden Street when a man in a grey car stopped," he replied. "He asked which way it was to Caldmore Green. We pointed up the street but he asked Christine to get in the car and show him the way."

"What happened next?" he asked.

"She got into the car," he replied.

"What happened after she got into the car?" he asked.

"It drove off," he replied. "But it went the other way and not towards Caldmore Green."

"Thank you," he said. "I have no further questions."

The other crucial witnesses were the ones who said they had recognised Morris as the man they had seen on Cannock Chase the day Christine was murdered.

Mrs. Nancy Daniel, of Stony Lane, Bloxwich was called to the witness box.

"Were you on Cannock Chase on Saturday the 19th of August, 1967?" Mr. Gibbens asked.

"Yes, I was," she replied.

"And what did you see?" he asked.

"I saw a man with a pretty child in his car," she replied.

"Can you see that man in court?" he asked.

"Yes," she replied, pointing to Morris. "He's the one in between the two police officers."

Mrs. Jean Rawlings, of Castle Croft Road, Wolverhampton, was next to take the stand.

"Can you tell the court what you saw on Saturday the 19th of August, 1967 on Cannock Chase?" he asked.

"My husband and I had gone to Cannock Chase that afternoon for a picnic," she replied. "I was getting out of the car with the dog when I heard the sound of a car approaching. I grabbed the dog so that the car could pass. It almost knocked me down."

"Is the man you saw driving the car that day present in this courtroom today?" he asked.

"Definitely," she replied. "He is the man standing in the dock."

Now it was Victor Whitehouse's turn.

"Could you tell the court your name?" Mr. Gibbens asked.

"Victor Whitehouse," he replied.

"And where do you live?" he asked.

"High Green Road, Hednesford," he replied.

"Could you tell the court what you were doing on Cannock Chase on Saturday the 19th of August, 1967?" he asked.

"Certainly," he replied. "I go for walks every day on the Chase. I know it like the back of my hand. That day I was walking my dog and saw a slate grey saloon car parked in a fire ride with a middle aged man standing beside it."

"And do you see that man in court today?" he asked.

"Yes," he replied. "It's the man over there in the dock."

There was pure mayhem outside as the highlight of the trial came.

Carol Morris was called to give evidence and the entire public wanted to witness it. After the last seat in the public gallery had been taken, there were still people outside trying to get in.

The ashen faced young woman in the witness box appeared completely different from the one who had been interviewed by Detective Chief Superintendent Forbes and Detective Chief Inspector Molloy a few weeks previously.

"Please take this in your right hand and speak the words written on the card," said the court usher, handing her the Bible.

Clinging to it, and not looking towards her husband, she said, "I swear by Almighty God to tell the truth, the whole truth, and nothing but the truth."

"Could you tell the court your husband's normal activities when he finished work on Saturday?" Mr. Gibbens asked.

Everybody in the room leaned forward to catch her quiet words.

"He usually finished work at one o'clock in the afternoon," she replied. "Before he came back home he would go and take the car to be washed."

"And where did he take it to be washed?" he asked.

"The car wash at Caldmore Green," she replied. "He'd arrive home about two o'clock."

"So you were aware of your husband's movements?" he asked.

"That's what he told me he did after work on Saturdays," she replied.

"Why did you lie to the police when your husband was questioned about his movements on Saturday the 19th of August?" he asked.

"I didn't lie," she replied. "I wasn't keeping quiet either. I just agreed with what he said."

"So on three separate occasions you were not only allowing to be said in your presence, but confirming, that he was shopping with you?" he asked.

"I didn't think he was the person responsible," she replied.

"You believed at the time that what you were telling the police officers was the truth?" he asked.

"I believed it because I couldn't believe he was the person connected," she replied.

"I'm sorry, Mrs. Morris but I don't understand what you are saying," interrupted the Judge. "Could you put it more clearly?"

"Yes," she replied. "I knew that what I was saying was untrue, but I couldn't believe it."

"You're still not making yourself very clear," the Judge said.

"It never occurred to me that there was anything sinister in the questions the police were asking him," she said.

"You knew perfectly well that your husband had arrived late home that day so you were misleading the police," the QC said.

"He told me he'd arrived home late because he had to stay behind to tell his boss what had been happening in the factory in his absence," she said.

"So why did you say something which was not so?" he asked.

"Because he came home and acted normal," she said. "He ate his meal and didn't show any sign of emotion about anything. I did not think he was the person concerned."

"What time exactly did he come home that day?" he asked.

"I would say between four and four thirty," she replied.

"Now," he said, "Let's go back to the night before bonfire night last year. What time did your husband arrive home that night?"

"It was just before eight o'clock," she replied.

"Did you look at the clock when he came home?" he asked.

"No," she replied.

"So how do you know it was about eight o'clock?" he asked.

"Because Coronation Street had just come to an end," she replied.

It was now time to be cross examined. She was having a rough ride.

"You have told my learned friend about what you told the police," Mr. Kenneth Mynett, QC, the defence counsel said. "You said that you agreed with what your husband had said because you couldn't believe he was responsible. Now you are saying you believed you were telling the police the truth?"

"Yes," she replied. "Because I didn't think he was connected with it."

"At that time did you know what time he had really got back home?" he asked.

"Yes. He got back at four thirty," she replied.

"You said you'd left a steak in the oven when you left your mother's house. How long would it take for you to get back to your flat from your mother's house?" he asked.

"About ten minutes," she replied.

"And how long was it before you had your meal when you got home?" he asked.

"It was as good as ready when we got back home," she replied.

"Do you happen to know what time it was when you had your meal?" he asked.

"It was probably between six and seven o'clock," she replied. "Because between eight and eight thirty we went out with my parents for a drink."

"That's all I need to ask, your Honour," he said, turning to the Judge.

"You can step down now, Mrs. Morris," the Judge said.

She let out a sudden sigh and her legs almost folded as she stepped down from the witness box.

Chapter 16

THE TRIAL WAS MAKING headlines all over the newspapers and was nearing its climax.

The next witnesses to take the stand were Morris's in laws.

Carol's mother had never liked him from the day he married her daughter. He'd crossed the line and she had never forgotten. She wouldn't rest until he was beaten, destroyed. She wanted him to suffer for what he was putting her daughter through. She wanted the vermin that attack children to be exterminated.

"Can you tell the court what happened on Saturday the 19th of August, Mrs. Horsley?" the QC asked.

Regardless of the glare from the people in the courtroom she was confident.

"I had forgotten to get some cakes when I was out shopping with Carol that morning," she said. "I asked her if she could get them for me when Ray got home. When they got to my house, it was after five o'clock; he told me he'd stayed behind at work to bring his boss up to date on what had been happening whilst he was away on holiday. That's why they were late getting the cakes. They dropped off the cakes and went straight back to their flat because Carol had to hurry home to get the steak out of the oven."

Carol's father took the stand.

"What time did your daughter and her husband arrive at your house on the 19th of August?" the QC asked.

"I'd been asleep," he replied. "Something told me it was time for the football results and I woke up and switched on the television. I can't be exact with the time, but they were coming to an end when my daughter and Ray walked in. I would say it was around a quarter past five."

Morris's boss was the next witness.

"Could you tell the court what time Mr. Morris clocked off from work on Saturday the 19th of August, 1967?" the QC asked.

"I have his clocking cards here with me," he replied, holding two cards up. "He clocked off at thirteen minutes past one on that Saturday."

"And what time did he clock out on the fourth of November, on the night of the attempted abduction?" he asked.

"At ten past seven in the evening," he replied.

Dr. Alan Usher, the Home Office Pathologist, who examined Christine's body, walked into the witness box with a face like stone. His movements were sharp and with purpose. He studied the jury for a few seconds then a fleeting smile flashed for just a moment. Behind the gun-metal spectacles his eyes were as grey as smoke and the lines around his mouth gave no indication that he lost himself in laughter.

"I went to examine the child's body at the scene and immediately could see that she had been the victim of a vicious attack," he said. "She was like a broken doll damaged beyond repair. At the mortuary I could see there were gaping and violent gashes in her genitalia. The person who committed the offence had most likely caused the damage with his fingers. She had been suffocated, probably by the pressure of a hand placed over her nose and mouth while she was being sexually assaulted. From my examinations of the body, it appears she died on August the 19th and the offence occurred at the spot where they found her."

"Was there any possibility that there may have been bloodstains on the assailant's clothes?" asked the QC.

"That is a very difficult question to answer," he replied. It depended on the position he took in committing the assault, but yes, it could have been bloodstained."

"I'd like Mrs. Morris to be recalled," the Mr. Mynett said.

She returned to the witness box.

"Do you wash your husband's clothes?" he asked.

"Yes," she replied.

"And did you see anything unusual on the clothes he had been wearing on Saturday the 19th of August; such as bloodstains."

"No, I didn't see any stains on his clothes," she replied.

"Thank you. That will be all," he said.

The expert from the Pirelli tyre company was next to give his evidence.

"In your opinion," said the QC. "Could you tell the court what type of tyre marks were found near the scene?"

"I couldn't identify the make of car from them," he replied. "But I would say they were the pattern and wheel base of a family car. I could see that the car had driven forwards or in reverse to where they found the body, and it had returned without being turned round."

The evidence about the murder had come to an end and the prosecuting counsel called on Mrs. Wendy Lane who had seen the attempted abduction on the eve of bonfire night.

"You saw the attempted abduction of a little girl on November the 4th last year, didn't you?" Mr. Gibbens asked.

"That's right," she replied.

"Can you tell the court what you saw?" he asked.

"I saw a man trying to push the girl into his car," she said.

"And why did you think he was trying to kidnap her?" he asked.

"I didn't think he was trying to kidnap her," she replied. "I thought there was something wrong because she was struggling with him, so I called out. He got in his car and drove off."

"Thank you," he said. "I have no more questions."

Looking at Mrs. Lane, the defending counsel asked, "You memorized the number plate, didn't you?"

"Yes," she replied. "I got the figures mixed up but they were the correct ones."

"You made a mistake," he said.

"No," she said. " I could actually see the numbers from the number plate at the back. They were illuminated, reflective ones."

"I understand that you also identified his car from twenty one others lined up in the police station yard?" he asked.

"Yes," she replied.

"Then why did you fail to pick him out at the identification parade?" he asked.

"Because he had his head down low when he drove past me," she replied. "And I couldn't see his face."

"Thank you. I have no further questions," he said.

The time had come for the prisoner to give his side of the story.

The courtroom buzzed with tension as the defence counsel, rose to his feet. His half-moon glasses perfectly balanced on the tip of his nose.

"Your Lordship, I call the accused, Raymond Leslie Morris."

A prison officer took Morris from the dock and led him to the witness box, standing guard at the foot of the steps.

He looked tired and had black rings under his eyes.

Taking the Bible in his right hand he said, "I swear by almighty God that the evidence I give will be the truth, the whole truth, and nothing but the truth."

"Did you use the words: 'Oh God, is it my wife? When you were arrested?" asked Mr. Mynett.

"No I didn't," he replied.

"Were you assaulted by the police while you were under arrest?" he asked.

"Yes," he replied.

"Is your wife telling the truth about the time you arrived home on Saturday the 19th of August?" he asked.

"No," he replied. "She's telling lies. Mr. Forbes told me that he'd seen her and she'd changed her statement and that she wanted nothing further to do with me."

The voice of a child rang out, breaking the silence of the court.

"That's him. That's the man who did it to me. Him down there," she yelled.

All heads turned to the public gallery.

A teenage girl, with her arm outstretched, was pointing down at the witness box and the accused man.

Morris looked up.

There was commotion in the gallery and a court usher quickly jostled her out.

The girl turned out to be Julia Taylor who had been raped and left for dead in December, 1964.

The prosecution counsel started its cross examination.

"How well do you know Cannock Chase?" Mr. Gibbens asked

"Not that well," he replied. "I've been there on several occasions."

"I'd like you to consider what happened to Christine Darby when she was being murdered," he said. "Your Honour, would you allow the accused to see the photographs of the victim?"

"Permission granted," he replied.

An usher handed them up to Morris.

"Whoever killed the child must have lifted her clothing above her waist and removed her plimsolls, must he not?" Mr. Gibbens asked.

"Yes, sir," he quietly replied.

"And the position of her body suggests that she could have been sexually assaulted?" he asked.

"Yes, sir," he replied.

The QC held up Christine's jeans and knickers.

"These would have had to be removed first, wouldn't they?" he asked.

"Yes, sir," he replied.

"I would like you to take a look at these photographs you took of your wife's niece," he said, handing him the album.

"Was your wife in the house when you took them?" he asked.

"Yes," he whispered.

"In the next room?" he asked.

"In the next but one room, sir," he replied.

The deadly quiet in the air, like a silent, creeping, numbing thick mist descended upon the courtroom like a black cloak of enveloping darkness.

"Tell me how it was you came to take these pictures?" he asked, turning his head and glancing at the jury.

"I was taking portraits of her, and she accidentally exposed herself as I took it," he replied, after a moment of thought.

"Are you telling the jury that the girl's posture in that picture is accidental?" interrupted the Judge.

"No, sir," he replied.

"Then what do you mean?" he asked.

"While I was taking the pictures," he replied. "I'm not sure whether she was leaning on the bed or lying on it but she fell backwards. I saw her like that and rearranged the position."

"I find this amazing," said Mr. Gibbens. "You have already pleaded guilty to indecently assaulting your wife's niece and now you are denying it."

He gave Morris another photograph.

"Look at this photograph," he said, handing it to him. "This photo shows the little girl fully dressed. She looks a happy little girl, doesn't she? She's smiling, isn't she?"

"Yes," he replied.

"Either you or the girl had raised her dress and under slip above her waist. Who did that?" he asked.

"I don't know," he replied.

"Why?" he asked. "When taking portraits of a five year old girl, was it necessary for you or her to raise her dress up in that position?"

"I'm not sure," he replied.

"Here are some more photographs of the child with her knickers on," he said. "When were those taken?"

"On the same day," he replied. "But after the others."

"Who asked her to put her knickers on?" he asked.

"I did, sir," he replied.

"Does she normally go about with no knickers?" he asked.

"No, sir," he replied.

Dread set on his face like rigor mortis and his teeth locked tightly together.

"I say no but I have no prior knowledge of this," he continued.

"I'd like you to take another look at the photo of Christine Darby's body," he said. "The position of her body bears an uncanny resemblance to the position of your wife's niece in her photos. Why did you take this photo of your wife's niece like that?"

"I didn't notice it was like that," he replied. "She may have leaned back."

"Do you notice certain things similar to the dead body?" he asked. "The dress is pulled up to the waist?"

"Yes, sir," he replied.

"Did you pull the dress up to her waist?" he asked.

"Yes," he replied.

"Did you want the girl in that position for the photograph?" interrupted the Judge.

"I would say yes, sir," he replied.

"Did you place the child in indecent positions for the other photographs in the set?" Mr. Gibbens asked.

"Yes," he replied.

"Let me ask you about the photograph that shows your penis next to the child's private parts," he said. "What was the purpose of doing this?"

"I still don't know," he replied.

"You don't know?" he asked. "You must know. Does the sight of a toddler with no knickers on arouse you?"

"I couldn't stop myself," he replied. "I got turned on and I was telling lies about saying that some of the poses were by accident."

"Can we agree that the photographs of your wife's niece were taken on August the 17th, 1968?" he asked. "That was within two days of the anniversary of the death of Christine Darby, wasn't it?"

"Yes," he replied.

"Were you recreating what you had done with Christine Darby a year before?" he asked.

"I didn't know Christine Darby, sir," he replied.

"What you did to your wife's niece in the photograph was in some respects the same thing that must have happened with Christine Darby?" he asked.

"I don't quite follow what you are saying," he replied.

"You said you felt disgusted with yourself after you took the pictures, yet you went to the extent of photographing yourself doing so," he said. "Can you explain that?"

"No. I can't," he replied.

"Isn't the explanation is that you have a lust for little children?" he asked.

"That isn't true," he replied.

The Judge interrupted again.

"When you came out of the bedroom after taking photographs of your wife's niece, did you tell your wife what you had done?" he asked.

"No," he replied.

"Did you enjoy it?" asked the Judge.

"I don't know what to say," he replied. "It was just something I had done. I'd never taken pictures like that before and I didn't think."

"Did the little girl enjoy it?" he asked.

"I wouldn't know, sir," he replied.

The Judge's knuckles turned white as he clenched his fist and banged it down hard on his bench. "Oh yes you would," he said. "Tell the jury."

His face slid into a hint of apocalypse. "I just don't know," he said.

"Can you tell me why you were wearing your wrist watch around your right ankle when you arrived at Winson Green Prison?" asked Mr. Gibbens.

"I just kept it on," he replied. "It was something personal I wanted to hang on to."

"Oh my giddy aunt," he said. "Do you expect me to believe that?"

"You can believe it or not," he replied.

"Were you anxious after the police saw you that your wife would withdraw her support about your movements on the 19th of August?" he asked.

"It would look bad for me if she changed her mind," he said. "But I never said Oh God, is it my wife to the police."

"I have no more questions, My Lord," said Mr. Gibbens.

The prison officer took Morris back to the dock.

It was all over.

Chapter 17

IT WAS THE 17th of February, 1969. The seven day trial had come to an end. The four year murder hunt had come to an end. All that was left were the closing speeches from the Prosecution and Defence, the Judge's summing up, and the verdict from the jury.

The verdict would bring a closure for Christine Darby's family but would it be a closure for the families of Margaret Reynolds and Diane Tift?

Mr. Brian Gibbens, QC, for the prosecution stood up and looked directly at the jury.

"I suggest that Morris's cry on arrest was that of a man who had been left by the only person who could support his alibi and who had since told you that the alibi was false," he said. "If she was deliberately lying to you, can you imagine anything more evil than that? Is she telling you the truth and holding herself under control, or is she committing one of the most evil forms of perjury that we have heard of in these courts?"

Mr. Kenneth Mynett, QC, defending, stood up and walked over towards the jury.

"The Crown is endeavouring to support what is a pretty weak case so far as identification is concerned by introducing that series of revolting, disgusting photographs taken by this man about a year after the murder. It has, unhappily, inevitably created very deep prejudices. As far as the similarities between the photographs and the murder there is no similarity between the cases. You, the jury, will have to contend with the black, overwhelming, suffocating prejudice created in your minds by the introduction of those photographs."

He turned and looked directly at Morris's wife.

"Mrs. Morris had altered her story after fifteen months," he said. "I am suggesting for your consideration that where Mrs. Morris realized the implications of her evidence, where she knew she was hurting her husband, she was lying on oath. Where she did not realise the implications, she might be telling the truth. That is a matter for you to decide – how far to trust that woman's evidence."

The Judge, Mr. Justice Ashworth looked down at the jury.

"No one can doubt that someone abducted and murdered Christine Darby and someone had attempted to abduct the other little girl in circumstances outlined by the prosecution. The man standing in the dock is accused of the murder of Christine Darby and the attempted abduction of another girl. I must warn you not to lump the charges together. You have to consider each separately and to deliver a separate verdict. It would be quite wrong to say that if he did one he must have done the other. You must also judge the photographs strictly in context of identity and not allow yourselves to be swayed by a natural outrage. You have to consider whether there was a hallmark or trademark linking the events. You have to be sure before you can convict the accused of anything."

He looked down at his papers, paused, and then looked back at the jury.

"Serious allegations have also been made by the accused man about his treatment by the police. If at the end of the day you are sure these charges against the police are unfounded, it must follow that he is telling lies and you are searching for the truth. You also have to take into consideration the evidence given by the two witnesses who saw the accused on Cannock Chase on the day of the murder. What made Mrs. Morris change her story on the 15th of November? It wasn't the filthy photographs, because the police had not yet found them. Was it the fact that the accused had previously been questioned in connection with the attempted abduction? In any event, Mrs. Carol Morris had told lies. I say that without hesitation. Either she lied originally in confirming his alibi or she is lying now. You should approach her evidence with very considerable reservation. Members of the jury it is now time for you to retire and consider your verdict."

The group of nine men and three women were led out of the courtroom and into a small room which was guarded by a court usher.

No one knows what goes through a jury's minds as they deliberate in private. They are all complete strangers to one another and come from different walks of life. They don't think like police officers or lawyers. They have listened to the trial from all aspects and have taken instructions from the Judge. It is now up to them to make the final decision.

The hands of the plain old clock on the wall never moved; it was like it was stuck in the same minute of the same hour for the longest time.

The knock came quietly.

The usher opened the door and cocked his ear to an unseen whisper. He closed the door, turned and nodded to the Clerk of the Court.

It was 4.28 pm and the jury was coming back. They'd been out for one hour and forty minutes.

"Have you elected a foreman?" the Clerk asked.

"We have," the jury replied.

The foreman stood up.

"Have you reached a verdict?"

"We have," he replied.

"Do you find the defendant, Raymond Leslie Morris, guilty or not guilty of the charge of attempted abduction?"

"Guilty," he replied.

"And of the murder of Christine Darby?"

"Guilty," he replied.

Cheers erupted from the public gallery like an auditory volcano. One second it was quiet and then deafening the next.

"Silence in court, please," the Clerk said.

When word of the verdict had reached the crowd outside, they started to chant: "Hang him. Hang him."

Morris's eyes sunk and he almost toppled over as he took a step backwards.

The Judge couldn't pass the death sentence because it had been abolished in 1965.

Looking at him directly, Mr. Justice Ashworth said, "I do not intend to keep you long or make any comment about this terrible murder. There is only one sentence as you know. Life imprisonment."

He felt as if an invisible force was turning his body to stone. An ache in his lungs made him realize that he wasn't sure whether or not he was breathing. He willed his limbs to move but they stayed as still as stone. For a fleeting moment he thought he'd become a statue.

He turned with vigour, walked across the dock and took two steps down towards the cells. Then he stopped. For a few seconds his eyes moved like a missile across the public gallery until they fixed onto his wife. Only he knew what thoughts were going through his tormented mind.

As Morris disappeared down the steps to the cells, the Judge said, "There must be many mothers in Walsall and the area whose hearts will beat more lightly as a result of this verdict."

Conclusion

CANNOCK CHASE IS THE smallest area of outstanding natural beauty in England and is the jewel of the West Midlands. It consists of pine forest and heathland and is very popular with cross country mountain bikers, picnickers, and campers alike.

Since the murders there have been claims of people witnessing black-eyed children roaming the forest and believe that they are the tormented souls of the murder victims.

Sixty years have passed since the murder of Carol Ann Stephens in Cardiff, and over fifty years have passed since Raymond Leslie Morris, infamously known as the Cannock Chase murderer, was convicted of Christine Darby's murder.

He was never found guilty of the murders of Margaret Reynolds and Diane Tift even though their bodies were found on Cannock Chase. They had been abducted and died under similar circumstances.

There was no DNA in those days but there is DNA today. Surely the police must have samples of Morris's DNA. There must be some way that laboratories can use this information to see if he was guilty of the other murders which still remain unsolved on police records. Surely something can be done to bring a closure for the relatives of Margaret Reynolds and Diane Tift, and maybe Carol Stephens.

Morris continued to maintain his innocence, but after he was arrested there were no more child abductions or child murders in the area.

The hunt for the Cannock Chase killer was the biggest murder hunt in British history.

In 2010 he was granted a judicial review to refer his case to the Court of Appeal in a bid to overturn his conviction. It was rejected.

He died in prison, handcuffed to his bed, in March 2014, after serving 45 years. He was 84 years old.

His crime was murder. His victims' crimes were being little girls.

The End

A note from the Author

I WOULD BE GRATEFUL if you would give this book an honest review.

Thank you.

Acknowledgments

I WOULD LIKE TO GIVE thanks to the following media for helping me with my research into information for this book:

Express and Star, Wolverhampton.

The Guardian.

Newspapers.com

Don't miss out!

Visit the website below and you can sign up to receive emails whenever David J Cooper publishes a new book. There's no charge and no obligation.

https://books2read.com/r/B-A-CBBF-RTLDB

BOOKS 2 READ

Connecting independent readers to independent writers.

Did you love *Cold Fury*? Then you should read *The Devil Knows*[1] by David J Cooper!

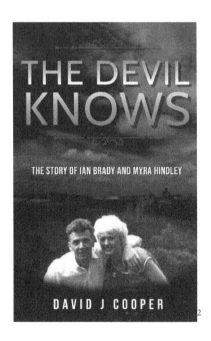[2]

A perverse couple who wanted to commit the perfect crime.....

In the early 1960s, residents of Manchester, England were horrified by the sadistic murders of five local youngsters between the ages of 10 and 17. Known as The Moors Murders, the perpetrators of the crime spree—Myra Hindley and Ian Brady—showed absolutely no remorse for what they had done, nor did they serve up any explanation for why they targeted their particular victims. Upon conviction, the pair received

1. https://books2read.com/u/47xx8j

2. https://books2read.com/u/47xx8j

consecutive life sentences rather than execution, the death penalty having been abolished a few months before their arrest.

This book is about their perverse relationship and how they lured their victims to their horrible deaths.

Will the body of Keith Bennett ever be found?

Are there other bodies buried on the moors?

Buy The Devil Knows today if you would like to know what makes a seemingly normal couple want to commit such heinous crimes.

Read more at davidjcooperauthorblog.wordpress.com.

Also by David J Cooper

Penny Lane, Paranormal Investigator
The Witch Board
The House of Dolls
The House of Dolls
The Devil's Coins
The Mirror
The Key
The Reveal

Standalone
Foul Play
The Devil Knows
The Party's Over
Penny Lane, Paranormal Investigator. Series, Books 1 - 3
Encuentro Mortal
Se Acabo La Fiesta
Cold Fury

Watch for more at davidjcooperauthorblog.wordpress.com.

About the Author

David J Cooper is a British author. He was born in Darlaston, West Midlands, to a working class family. After leaving school he had jobs ranging from engineering to teaching. He got involved in local politics and became a local councillor in 1980.

His novels incorporate elements of the paranormal, horror, suspense, and mystery.

He is featured in the Best Poems and Poets of 2012 with his first and only poem God's Garden.

He currently lives in a small town in Mexico with his three dogs, Chula, Sooty, and Benji.

Read more at davidjcooperauthorblog.wordpress.com.

Made in the USA
Monee, IL
29 August 2020